Transplant
Transport
Transubstantiation

Transplant
Transport
Transubstantiation

Poems by Marjorie Maddox

WIPF & STOCK · Eugene, Oregon

Wipf and Stock Publishers
199 W 8th Ave, Suite 3
Eugene, OR 97401

Transplant, Transport, Transubstantiation
By Maddox, Marjorie
Copyright©2004 by Maddox, Marjorie
ISBN 13: 978-1-5326-5512-8

Publication date 8/1/2018
Previously published by WordTech Editions, 2004

for the donor
of my father's heart

for my mother,
who kept our hearts going

for Gary, Anna Lee, and Will,
who keep my heart full

Acknowledgements

American Literary Review, "Disconnected," "Seagulls" (nominated for a Pushcart Prize).

Anglican Theological Review, "Divorce"

Anthology of Magazine Verse and Yearbook of American Poetry, "Somewhere in Yugoslavia"

Anthology on Parenting, "Flight Patterns"

Ascent, "Walking the Same Way Everyday"

Blueline, "Maple Seed: A Love Poem"

Body Parts (Anamnesis Press Chapbook), "Body Parts"

Christian Century, "The Waiting Room"

Christianity and Literature, "The Sacred Heart of Jesus"

Confrontation, "When She Moves Beside Me"

Crab Orchard Review, "After Your Transplant"

Dominion Review, "At the British Museum," "How It Begins"

Ecclesia (Franciscan University Press Chapbook), "Ash Wednesday," "Divorce," "Eucharist," "The Sacrament of Penance," "The Sacred Heart of Jesus"

Essential Love (PoetWorks), "Flight Patterns"

Exit 13, "Center St."

Exquisite Differences, "The Lung"

Fathers: A Collection of Poems (St. Martin's Press, David Ray, ed.), "Old Tunes"

First Things, "Ash Wednesday," "The Sacrament of Penance," "Treacherous Driving"

Gulf Stream, "Transplant, Transport, Transubstantiation"

How to Fit God into a Poem (Painted Bride Chapbook), "Magnificat"

Image: A Journal of the Arts and Religion, "Eucharist"

International Quarterly (finalist for 1995 Crossing Boundaries Award), "Skin Rising"

Jane's Stories II: An Anthology by Midwestern Women, "Old Tunes"

Karamu, "My Mother Gives Me a Tape of My Father's Dance Band"

Knowing Stones: Poems of Exotic Places (John Gordon Burke Publisher, Inc.), "Cape"

Montserrat Review, "Hip," "My Mother Gives Me a Tape of My Father's Dance Band"

Northeast Corridor, "Anniversary Poem Interrupted with a Fight"

The Other Side, "Ribs"

Painted Bride Quarterly, "After Learning of Our Own Deaths," "Body and Soul," "Magnificat"

Pinyon Poetry, "Cowper's Glands," "The Gall Bladder," "The Kidneys," "The Pancreas"

Perpendicular As I (Sandstone; Author's Guild Backinprint.com Edition), "Ribs"

Phrases After Noon (chapbook by Robert Hass and Eric Trethewey), "Somewhere in Yugoslavia"

Radix, "The Sacrament of Marriage"

Rattapallax, "The Pericardium"

Salmon Magazine, "Years Later: His Funeral"

Tar River Poetry, "Somewhere in Yugoslavia"

The Women's Review of Books, "Tape of My Dead Father's Voice on an Old Answering Machine"

Windhover, "Magnificat"

Whiskey Island Magazine, "When You Talk"

Thanks also to Lock Haven University, for an Alternative Workload Leave; Andrew Hudgins and Ellen Bryant Voigt, for insightful critiques of this manuscript in its earlier versions; the Virginia Center for the Creative Arts, for space to write many of these poems; the poetry group in Lewisburg, for Sunday afternoon guidance; my family, for their support; and my husband, Gary, for everything—and more.

Contents

I.

Treacherous Driving

"It's as safe as traveling to work . . ."
                    — a cardiologist before performing a transplant

The first night of the blizzard,
that stranger inched into Ohio.
Halfway through he skidded
into our snow–spackled lives.
His heart is buried
in my father,
who is buried.

This is the hole
in the stranger, in my
father, in my own
cracked chest, hail cupped in its cavity,
the aorta beginning to freeze.

All winter,
the weather preaches white
lies: fields blank of roads,
a curve straightened,
the even light of sky.

Tonight the breeze is all
icicles, banner–like
from the clouds. Nothing
is moveable
in this treacherous state.

Our wheels spin,
their rhythm: a breath
that pulls us
then stalls. The law

of the body, of the state,
cannot replace the chain
reaction, jackknifed lives,
hope piling into hope.

The man and his heart,
cold on an icy road,
warmed us for weeks
while winter, a clear blue thing,
wafted light.

Disconnected

"The heart has its own nervous system . . . [once transplanted, it]
can beat independently of the brain."
— *The Boston Globe Magazine*

Its nerves left dangling,
so many severed cords
uncoiled and floundering
about uninsulated space
I think—until a priest–turned–
surgeon explains in stops and shocks
the transubstantiation of transplants,
what others' hearts were, are, continue to become
inside our opened hollows,
disconnected from used nerves
that bridge to blood.

Instead, this always–symbol,
always–physical of personage
completes itself, confidently connecting
to what it needs, its sinoatrial node
part of that separate
chambered system of someone else,
heart of the fact that keeps it still
believing what it does.

In the transplant waiting room,
a child asks her mother,
"Will Daddy love the same people?"
and I startle at the complications.

While the slow clock sterilizes
the lives of those waiting shock–still
or nervous–twitching,

I think, out–of–time, of persons whom I've become
on stage, transforming what I wasn't into
what I wasn't.

In seventh grade, the penalty for breaking
character in Theater class was failure.
And so we sat obediently as old women
but staring boldly, disconcertingly
back–and–forth at the blushing prop boy,
the unplugged cord, when,
in *Arsenic and Old Lace*,
the telephone kept ringing, ringing, ringing.

The Waiting Room

does not wait patiently
for us, its stucco walls vacant
of the pain we hang upon the gray
and graying we soon become. Between,
we pretend to plan a son's
baptism, book revisions, a summer life that lives after
this. Your husband wants a liver;
I want a heart that breathes an average rhythm
within my father's ribs. The others here
won't fit into our tight, cramped list
of miracles and what we need
to get there. Behind our prayers:
the backdrop of another family winning
what they've lost, their stuttered cares,
the infection and rejection on our cross.

Landscape and Still Life

After the new heart, when blood
cultivated fungus in my father's fingers,
began harvesting his legs,
pruning flesh from the rotting fruit
of what we were
once, we too withered, lost
the way to move
in the moving world.

What would he photograph
now? we asked, he who walked miles
to catch light in its pedestrian way.

When, without fingers, he focused his lens,
framed and balanced unruly compositions,
subjects sprouting onto film,
how would his body's landscape separate
lights and darks, begin
again to develop?

Masked and scrubbed
in the half–light of intensive–care,
we study his absences,
the silhouette of appendages
lost, phantoms tucked neatly
beneath the photo–screen of sheets.
Obedient still–lives, we stay and stay
until he, too, is gone.

After Your Transplant

The heart, those four walls of clichés,
creak in on me like Disney's
haunted home. Mid–summer your name,
arrhythmic, still clatters in my veins.
Like yours, my bloody pump now leans
this way and that. I wake dismayed
that I still wake. The ordinary trains
for ordinary: day estranged
from day, the overarching aim
of light on blank expanse. This pain,
mundane in its display
of what is wrong and mean, reclaims
belief in miracles, the sane
or insane wish you misnamed
prayer. And yet, you plotted, risked it,
with faith—not luck, not superstition,
waiting for what finally came
from someone dead. The counterclaim
is that from death came death, a game
of synonyms, of metaphrase
that interchanged malaise
with thumping grief. There is no name
for what you couldn't get. A man
gave you his heart. Unashamed,
you took it. At a distance,
you followed where he'd gone. To listen
to your heart, you need one. To refrain
from hope? The same as arteries, veins
so bloated, clogged, they can't contain
a bit of life. You undid cliché:

the heart worked; the blood alone decayed.
Foreknowledge gone into another room,
the walls move in—the dying die too soon.

After My Father's Death: A Week on the Lake

Even in dark, a hole un–
seams larger. Light,
once shipwrecked, seaweed–stubborn, lets
its liquid go, filaments
unfrosting in the portal.
What ungripping of submission
not torn but worn
out, away into the gaping lack
that lets us see. And sometimes
sound: lines loosed and looping into,
out of the nicked vision that splinters
seldom, thin as split threads,
into hope. It is your voice
that ventures so low, uncloses
the opening, the dark and undone
re–twined into one vast, vacant
glow: and this death (the separating, the whole)
cannot float me, cannot let me go.

Bury Our Heart

Like every other,
this is the year of shifting
sorrows, the thin shadows of land
that slip from countries we've left
for fear or want
of finding ourselves
in a handful of dirt.

Even in sleep,
a warm wonder of birth and loss,
there too the earth's vibrations,
the leveling of cliffs in eyes we claim.

The soul is the land
liquid in the lines of veins
that stripe the inner atlas.
It bubbles and flows, smoothes
the rough roads, carves out
our caves of refuge,
our weeping echoes.

Here too, they will find us:
the outcasts, the fugitives,
the lost, the abandoned,
the running–for–our–lives.

O homeland of sadness,
these dusty bones that could not save.
I have held in my clay hands,
the fine grains of his blood,
bold in my muddy palms;

I have held in my earthen arms
the jagged pot of his pain,
brimming and bitter.

      I have waited
for that open mouth
of the world
to lay him down.

Framing My Father's War Roster
Just Before Memorial Day

He survived
the shells but not the stranger's
heart unshelled on the surgeon's table,
stitched into his own black pit
two years before this year's fiftieth celebration
of endings and surrenders.

To frame his name is more
than a month's pay of his combat,
but a tiny cell compared to the transplant
expense enlisted by insurance.

"The torn edges make it more authentic,"
my mother says, and I agree,
listening for valves that can't close
on this disintegrating, jagged poster
once plastered on a hometown post office
before my father ripped it down:
would–be souvenir for a son.

But my brother got the watch
after the present from his wife.
(He only said, "Oh, I just got one.")
My mother kept the medals.

I still have the name
inserted before the new
like this roster behind unbreakable,
fire–resistant glass within an antique–
looking frame that matches my grandmother's hope
chest, my great–aunt's rocking chair
in the living room where we live.

"Sudden Death"

In medical reports, the term used to describe
a heart that suddenly stops beating

Makes me see
two boys balancing, one bare foot before the other,
fast now, slow, on railroad tracks, their toenails dirty.
From behind: a charred–gray engine burning up the air
but silently, as if a cartooned villain
with smoky cape scripted unread warnings.
Even open–mouthed passengers struck dumb,
and both boys impossibly
too preoccupied to sense the doom.
I forget about the track's vibrations and common sense,
the way fear amputates all facts we give away to others.

And if not that definition—"Sudden Death":
two battered Buicks on a pot–holed road
out in Wisconsin or western Pennsylvania;
the cars are hacking hard the way my uncle choked on steak
and called his wife, and then the whole family
took turns smacking to get the gristle out.
And wait, the cars are aiming at each other,
coming out of different skies and lives. There's purpose here,
at least intent. To kill
or scare to death. But is it sudden? That second
where you turn away or toward
is what your life was leading to.

But I am leading somewhere else instead—
the way the words "Sudden Death"
typed up in these reports from hospitals in different states
equal my father, six time survivor of the term
(Where's the seventh life?) that sent us crashing

into what we are. One day the heart wakes up and says,
"I've had enough" and stops its drone of work,
or maybe pauses just enough
to make us pause,
until it's finally lured into a life
that deaf and dumbly balances on tracks
as flat as monitors. Sudden Death

is what we resurrect from
uneasily, electric healers from which we steal belief
or not, the jolt that joins us at the organs.
Two days before my father's heart stopped dead,
again, then, hacking, started up,
my first–time husband–friend, caught in the electricity
of what he feared in others, cut clean
our ventricles, then began to stitch and pick
out, simultaneously, all track–like sutures.
And when I turned my half–heart toward
and then away, I knew only what was left
of engines, pumping lopsidedly away
those two boys who had hopped inside
to watch the battered Buicks rushing by.

II.

The Sacrament of Marriage

I. as baptism

Wet this wonder of will–be,
this hole of hope, brim–full and poured
on our bodied souls, this ecstatic cleansing
sinless and sanctioned. O, Solomon sing louder!
Aria of rivers, curved limbs, shores of skin,
mellifluent unction, sweet healing of liquid,
fully immersed in this sprinkle

of symbol flowing our yes and no,
the hard edges of bone; this christened ocean
of union, the blessed affusion, *Agnus Dei*'s streaming
across the uplifted, eyes inlands of prayer;
the bright bowl of our bondage

and deliverance, high in the arch of light,
in this Pentecost of pleasure, this divine bestowment:
your spirit in me, infusionism become human.

II. as confirmation

yes and yes and yes
chosen and spoken.
Beloved wedding guest's,
the Spirit's, token

of wisdom, knowledge,
counsel, holy fear,
true godliness, strength
consummate in years

of doubts, questionings,
yet unbroken creeds:
these worn wedding rings—
our gold string, prayer beads

of matrimony.
Up front and aloud,
we cite the "I believe . . . ,"
confirm our vows.

III. as eucharist

My body for you, my blood,
iron–poor but flowing
into your veins still bloated on red–cells,
my blood for you, my body,
creaking and open, bending and broken,
my hair, my ribs, my teeth, my lungs, my arms, my heart,
my toes, my liver, my breasts, my knees, my sex, my kidneys.

Take. Take. Take. Take. Take.

IV. as orders

This
is the house that
God built. This is the bishop.
This is the priest. This is the deacon.
This is the father. This is the mother. This is the child.
obeyobeyobeyobeyobeyobeyobeyobey
obeyobeyobeyobeyobeyobeyobeyobey
obeyobeyobeyobeyobeyobeyobeyobey
obeyobeyobeyobeyobeyobeyobeyobey
obeyobeyobeyobeyobeyobeyobeyobey
obeyobeyobeyobeyobeyobeyobeyobey
obeyobeyobeyobeyobeyobeyobeyobey
obeyobeyobeyobeyobeyobeyobeyobey

V. as penance

Like Peter's, our feet stink:
dusty, shit–stained, fish–smelling.

This day–to–day
one–foot–in–front–of–the–other ritual
cripples rigid bones, leaves us
hobbling: stubbed joy, twist of promise,
the blistering steps of hurt and heal.

And so we kneel,
with tattered sponges washing
the road from our soles
and ankles, each holding up
worse sores, each confessing
the muddied and clear; administering
sacred balm in the clean light
of an average kitchen.

VI. as extreme unction

And in the dying:
the howls and silence of the always–ill,
laments for the loss of the once loved,
the minutes misunderstood as misery.
What is undone in the unforgiving
are the alms of the everyday,
the laying on of hearts.

Too long the cup cracked,
the crusts of bread molding on the counter,
a trail for rodents.

Anoint and save, blessed Savior,
this failure to sustain
a sacrament breathed–out, sick of spirit,
and ready too late to right its life
in this the last–chance
miraculous rite.

Heredity

Before the E.R. doctor pronounced you
alive and partly well at 5:00 a.m., a stuffy morning
in July, when earlier even I, on the other side of our bed,
felt the pressure of your blood tighten
in my constricted dreams; before your father's
chest, sawed open like a rotting tree,
and all the sawdust sifted to your genes;
before your mother's warning stroke, my father's heart extracted
from a stranger, or the mastectomy
that made my mother whole,
before that 5:00 a.m. when all I feared began again
almost, the failures of our parents' bodies
pooling up inside us,

I loved and love the vows within your voice,
the loyalty of chromosomes passed on to child,
the DNA and discipline of doing
that faithful day–to–day of what is half–inherited,
the nucleus we nurture into love,
each parent cell a paradox,
reproducing through division
what we have and will become.

Maple Seed: A Love Poem

As children we called them "whirligigs,"
half wings of brittle leaf
seeded down with spin
click–clicking the air like a week of cicadas
hurled into our midst
by fists of trees tired of clenching
such drunken dancers.

We could only fling out
our arms; with their whole selves
whipping within the molecules of wind,
they pitched to–and–fro our hearts, hope, our half–wish always
for death dizzy as the dawn exhaled by the first day of summer
senselessness and sorrow. Or joy.

Plague–like, they play the breeze for a buffoon,
banter and clamor increasingly, then settle
seconds later on my hair, book, in the glass
of orange juice I raise
to such swift churning.

This is the frenzy of our faith no longer
frenzied, the fine filaments
of what clips us from the other,
from each other, and lets the twirl slow,
the not–final floating that lets love sprawl
on the green grass,
grow, spin, fall, grow.

Anniversary Poem Interrupted With a Fight

I.
All morning, I write love poems.

II.
Truth chisels its half–likeness, stands back and stares.
How often can words pray without answer,
without the confirmation of Amen? I believe
in paper and type, the shifting of symbol and space,
silhouettes of what we are.

III.
What we are

IV.
If we sit long enough in our separate rooms,
at our separate desks, at our separate words,
it will get dark, it will stay quiet,
it will

When You Talk

You push voice between syllables.
What sticks between the teeth is me.
From this you pick what you can.
And though nothing is what you know,
it slips in and steals details:
his socks, the last ten years,
cracked light bulbs in the lamps,
ten half–eaten breakfasts,
a decade of minutes sectioned,
sliced up with a serrated knife like
this. That plate that shines his face.
A chip at the edge the ivory of
dried skin. Even your last bit of voice too thick
on anything his.

11/11/89*

What I try to climb over is
(even here) nothing new: you
cutting sky with your hand;
shadows cross eye,
a palm too light to hold anything mine:
this side *dein Herz, deine Seele*,
sliced, served up, steam that won't sizzle through
or over. And still I'm unwalling
you into cracks the size of caverns,
the gray in your mouth,
something like voice falling through
and out. Stones. Splinters.
Bricks my tongue can't lick together.

*date the Berlin Wall came down

Center St.

In this neighborhood, someone is practicing the piano,
the drums, the baton, the cha–cha–cha–cha on the front lawn,
the "Heel before I kick you" with the dog,
and love. I am ecstatic with the click
of a ten–speed outside the window,
a gas pedal vroomed to the floor,
and the squirrel in your voice.
The would–be pianist now plays
a record and listens to the grooves
we are moved toward, not in.
She is listening to the absence of herself
or to us or rather the nothing between
the note we wish on, a voice that picks and chooses
which word to move in
or over. We are not the ones in love
but will be when the baton drops,
the aproned dancers turn,
or the terrier runs toward the tires,
and rhythms start and stop and start,
drumming this noise of ritual that keeps us
practicing what we may
or may not become.

Teaching Summer School Two Years After

All day birds pick worms from this earth,
two–step among the weeds.
Even dry ground has meat
and memory, a place for feet and beak,
and what is left of our lives.

A feather is a fine find
between the blades of what is
says the robin leaving
with wings full of weather.

We don't leave.
Worms slither the worry we slurp.
We cannot unlearn digestion.

Always what is small startles.
On the sidewalk: two half–formed
birds flattened into a grief
translucent as ours. I step over
them to teach metaphysics to freshmen
who refuse to flunk.

And you, child, curled
in your small box,
never forgetting to breathe
us back to your brief year,
you cling to their queries:
a question mark,
a fetus.

Walking the Same Way Every Day

It's the same as always: he's walking
down, I up. But this time, the man on Seneca
clacks his cane across the sidewalk toward
me, like the blind dividing traffic with a tap.

For weeks I've watched him half–heartedly,
foreground, background. Last Monday,
he clattered past a blue house;
a woman wide as morning leaned out
her second–story window, whistling
"Springtime in Paris."

Wednesday, gray hat perched like a baseball cap,
he patted a stray tabby by the mailbox
where I drop postcards.

He won't stay in the corner of my eye,
this old man, a detail in a picture you send
to show someone something else: white squirrel,
sunrise, construction you've complained about for weeks.

Today, he wants nothing but to see
me, me to see him and the stark joy of
orange: a leaf just to the right of my shoulder.

So, a small squirrel

springs from the neighbor's kitchen
with a bagel, what of it?
And maybe the garbage truck
has a dog in it
beneath the tin cans and coffee grounds,
but I'm talking about that lady
bug slipping past the arch of your
eyebrows and how much
this tea costs at competitive stores
and how many sips you'll take
to finish the cup.

Badminton Net

Though we rarely play,
we leave the net up when it rains,
the sagging lines reminders of what
in us divides and unifies. Behind it
(or in front, depending on your side),
a squirrel prostrates himself
against the yard's one oak and chatters
prayer, or, perhaps, new rules
to this game we do not play. Prayer, games,
even now I cannot take the other side and say
they are the same, that one begets the other
or divides to twins so alike
the mother may, for seconds at a time, forget
which one is which, unless, side by side,
they strike out with some different rhythm.
Still, our neighbors say, even this net
could catch our prayers and games,
pull itself up, and toss them into sky
like all our plastic birdies gone awry,
and there would be no difference in our lives.
On this we're unified: we pound the stakes in
deeper, talk about retying
the net, about playing.

Magnificat

I, too, chalked you with wings and horns
on my bathroom wall.
I pierced your left lobe with a halo
bent from the forked poker
of a neighbor's fire.
Even now, your eyes are like mine:
horrified and knowing.
What is there to see
but dust flicking into light,
my cells a kaleidoscope?
I'm tripping on veins,
am tied up by your tongue
that, yes, *is* connected to skull, breath, soul
buried somewhere beneath what's left
of the boiled and boned.
What is real tastes so
and smells
of everything in and out of living.
Your fingers let me suck salt;
your lungs lift the hush from my throat;
your feet take in the floor's splinters.
Here in my house, where I want you,
we tremble together.

III.

Body Parts

The Lung

A miniature stingray, it glides
only inside its bone cage,
slate–gray and shiny,
sliding about its domain, inhaling
anything within breath: the wind,
whispers, wild weeping, the way
a man walks through the winter air
toward a frozen pond,
a pole, a cigarette.

He looks down through the hole
in the ice and sees the stingray,
or its memory, circling the dark cold
of his body. What does it take to breathe
in or out? To keep
the poisonous spine swishing
in such chilly waters
about the heart?

The Pericardium

It hangs entwined in the branches of vessels—
a wasp's nest buzzing with breath,
but smooth as sap around the muscle.
Everything it holds
we hold dear. A fibro–serous
sack for the soul; a bagpipe of blood;
a conical bowl of our hopeful content.
The weight of aorta and auricles sifts into this,
the veins unveiled above its double covering.
What we wish for the world

and ourselves is what we have
here, close,
holding the heart.

Ribs

talk
in curves:
bone against
bone in combat,
bone of my flesh:
tusks of charging
elephants, rainbows
bleached and broken,
ice in a church–way arch,
sled for slippery questions,
pointer for do's and don'ts,
cage of the heart, protector?
striped, brittle, and bent—
a thin, sagging bridge
with boards missing,
blackness beneath:
the fine bone line
that saves/
enslaves
us.

The Liver

lives to lecture geometry,
a right–angled triangular prism
with edges rounded off,
a popular university guest,
three–dimensions of tanned reddish–brown
eager for freshman questions.

And what a success—
between circumferences and calculations:
gall bladder bashing, jokes about the duodenum,
a tongue–in–cheek tour of the abdominal cavity.

The Big Cheese at the department's
booze–and–cheese reception,
he lingers to digest degrees of praise,
complimentary angles of compliments.

The largest gland in the body,
he still wedges into tight corners
of women, meticulously compares
planes and curves.

After six whiskeys,
the fellow swells and bellows,
half–lacerates his lobes,
then, turning gray,
stumbles to a local dive
with two national merit scholars.

The Gall Bladder

stoned,
disowned,
thrown with her baggage of bile
on the bloody street,
her pear body rotting and reeking.

The last lover of the liver,
splayed connective tissue
about her yellowed feet.

The Pancreas

a half–foot of dog's tongue licking the spleen clean,
slobbering over the stomach and jejunum,
its spit fluid chewing
half–finished cornflakes, raw Fig Newtons
rumbling in the small intestines.

How bad can its bite be?
a dish of cysts or cancer,
a jowl–full of jaundice.

But you, too, are a stray.
Let the glossi lap your leftovers,
salivate to its gland's content.
Pet its loyalty; give it a name.

Sticks, Stones, and Spleen

O red and white pulp,
ductless gland, large lymphoid structure,
fibrous seat of melancholy
filtering out feeling,
holding hostage all bloody
hope in the cupped palm of your corpuscles.

Now fevered, you weigh more than wailing
twins wishing on the nipples of a mother
limp with leukemia.
Puffing yourself large,
a peritoneum–clinging bomb,
you can't burrow behind the diaphragm
any longer. O stubborn sieve,
haywire symbol of sorrow,
sponge–faced simp,
take off your fibro–elastic coat,

roll up your sleeves;
I'm coming in swinging
steel: sterilized and sharp.

The Appendix

A worm wishing it were a boa,
it twists this way and that,
slithering into inflammation.
Greedy, its hollow swallows all
foreign objects, eats too much
shit. It is a master of melodrama,
spur–of–the–moment masochisms.
Macho, it know what it wants and gets it.
Manipulative, it whines, moans, mimics
Lady Macbeth, its Shakespearean groans
snaking intestines: "Out! Out! Out!"

Intestines

Which tip to take and curl,
which end to stake as beginning,
the hose hand–wound tight as a target.
Not the messy winding that it is,
behind and out of organs, a score of casing
twisted, squeezed stereotypically.

What sound does it make stretched out?
A squeaked whistle, a sneezing passage of wind
tacked in plastic. How does it rig
as a rope? It rips, splatters the self's waste
about you. Wholly unsatisfactory
as a noose.

The Kidneys

can tango, can cha–cha–cha
about the cavity. On warm winter days,
they may waltz. It's all
hereditary.

Sometimes,
one floats off by itself,
red with embarrassment,
bobbing about the peritoneum like a lost fetus.
There's nothing to do but wave farewells.

Those who don't refuse
fuse with a partner early;
a joint inner tube, they ride the fatty waves.

The widowed sit still on the shore,
emaciated, afraid, pumping out their sorrow
for a fluid day.

The Bladder

has had its bad days, but adjusts.
Empty, it's a cup fit for a pint,
later, a dish rounding up liquid.
Filled to the brim, it's the yellow belly of a chameleon
ready to burst.

Cowper's Glands

They could have been the peas
beneath the royal Serta Sleeper
stubbornly making that sweet maid
toss and turn into a princess.

But they belong to the prince,
tucked in discreetly above the urethra,
a small yellow glow to pee by.

The Tunica Vaginalis

The parachute that billows over
the small pond of fish,
inverts, dips in, draws itself up;
the handsome catch in the fine, shut sac,
preparing to spawn.

The Round Ligaments

A round clothesline, stretching
from uterus to labia majora,
muscular tissue lost in the folds
of what was already folded,
angled connections hung high
in the body's pleated sky.

Hair

sprouts everywhere,
its perennial bulbs buried above the brain's bald spots;
don't call it Hirsute–Helmet or Film of Fur.
Remember: it sniffs out sinus passages,
deciphers the Morse code of moles across the calf,
coffee–clutches about the ear and listens.
It is the all–time spy
planted surreptitiously as plaits or pigtails,
perms, hippie beards, unpublic pubic.
An unruly strand, it sneaks in on the lip,
nips at the nipple,
hovers about the hip as if on holiday.
It ignores "No Trespassing!" notices,

has pre–stamped passport, is privy
to all our countries: private and clothed.

The Hip

was never a hippie,
though it knows how to swing itself
low for love, set itself lustily against the establishment.
It invented dance and doesn't regret a step of the twist,
the drown, the monster mash, or mash potato.
It's a hand–hold, tease, sexy shelf,
riveting joint of ball–and–socket,
the only measure of slinky song
on a jazzy day.

Areola

Pale rose to doe–brown:
the body's home–test for first pregnancies.
How Sherlock and cohorts
succinctly discovered
who'd been where
before.

The Stomach

Still curvy at forty,
she knows, deep inside, she's a star
the caliber of Garbo or Davis.

Daily, she stares
admiringly in the mirror,
sucks herself in.

Even the slim
ads of Cher

or the choreographed contortions
she'd gladly endure for Oprah
would work her naturally
gastronomic talent
more.

She's grunted and groaned
her way onto centerfolds,
late nights, daytime soaps—
cheap exploitations:
second billing to a spoon and bottle,
a doctor in lab coat.

She is more than her digestive attributes,
she consoles herself,
smoothing her mucous membrane and noticing,
once again, its luxurious
honeycomb glow.

Closet Skeleton

just hangs there,
its dead centipede of a spine
inclined to nothing.
Discreet, it keeps its feet clean,
sweeps up after it eats any sweets
on the attic stairs.
But it rarely dares such extremes,
its "scandalous scenes" all grossly exaggerated:
one late–night on the town, a bottle of vodka.
Mostly it sleeps,
unseen by the fresh flesh
fiendishly fornicating
behind the door next door.

Spine

A thirty–three bred and bone businessman,
he stands up when you come in, aligns himself
with himself, maybe hums "Dry Bones,"
but seldom unhinges in public.
Well–mannered but reticent and sometimes sentimental,
he shuns moving days, snow shoveling, and kinky sex,
and runs from high cliffs, shallow lakes.
Accused often of being stiff, he's only misunderstood,
an aristocrat lifting groceries and garbage,
a coward unwilling to pick a bone
with just any bully walking,
with perfect posture,
down the street.

The Tibia and Fibula

"Flute" and "clasp," they hook together
music and muscle in the moving leg:
beauty of bone in motion.

At the tuberosites, they join, stretch down
daily with grace above ballerina feet.
Sleek but easily fractured, they long for the shin's ridge,

for the flesh that keeps them pivoting
within new notes, within well–choreographed,
Fonteyn and Nureyev pirouetting passions.

Elbows, Knees

Contortionists,
both bend to the occasion,
kneel and lean themselves into trapeze twists,
stacked torsos toppling beneath top tents,

limbs that trick testy tigers,
that snap back from cat's teeth.

They let us go
and go back to the narrow and straight,
then crack into the unexpected,
smack with hairlines along the bare bones
of what we can't take back.

Joiners extraordinaire,
they beg for pads, guards, backhands,
then pile, slide, and slice themselves onto stretchers.
They are the stars of the show, tendons flaring nightly
in great tall tales of splintered constellations.

Nail

During full moon, the lunula glows larger,
arcs within epidermis that juts past toe or finger.
Left to its own, the stiff skin snarls, sharpens, howls in the dark,
clear breath of wolfish night.

The Big Toe

a runaway thumb,
hitching a ride away from the fingers
to see the body,

gains only
balance—the macadam street,
the tightrope that teases it.

Uncommonly Cold

Skullcap fissured with frost, fingernails
of ice scraping the surface. The dura mater
doesn't matter much;
huddled about the brain's lost warmth,
it can't stop quaking.
The subdural space fills with shaking
until its membranes, too taut,
creak apart. Blood freezes
in the tiny pipes of the pia mater
or squeezes through in chunks
to ventricles while white and gray matter
gel and crust over
and the optic thalamus stiffens,
clicking SOS to the cortex.
The fissures of Rolando and Sylvias
crack cavern–like, and a sign is posted
beside the corpus callosum—
Beware: freezes before road—
or worse—Beware: bridge out.
Slick and sickly,
the cerebellum coughs and sneezes,
stingily hoards its medicine,
each hemisphere turning a cold shoulder
to the other and refusing to speak.

The Ear

Half a misshapen moth,
mention hair lit as florescent filaments and she's there,
steering herself beside birthmarks, behind sideburns,
around the corner from chin.

She can't see her twin,
scavenger–like, settling off–center on the other side,
but hears the flip–flap of landing.

Obsessed with clicks and bangs,
the sighs of horses, the raw holler of hospitals,
she slices and fillets the gray of whispers,
tornadoes of referees.

It is all worth more than sick silences,
but she misses that too.

On nights when thought streams past canals,
cascades over bones, she hears herself groaning,
a stolen throat thumping the tympanum.

Then its echo is a leach
slimming into the cochlea,
a bitter, tight circle of snail.

Where will its sound slip when sorrow stops curling,
when vibrations vow no voice–over?
Her swan–like rods swim ovals about her.
The pinna almost sways.

Only the *pianoforte* of Corti can calm her,
weighted just so, enough like the wind to sift her,
shake out the wrinkled woe, and lift her.

The Appendages of the Eye

eyebrows

stretched comma,
charcoal frenzied into sketch,
arched shades of integument;

too much or little and hands steal with snips;
or fingers curve a lip–like swerve,
centimeters below unlined
but lifted brow.

eyelids

movable folds:
ride up to the first floor,
down to the basement;
solicitous, elevator muscles
wipe feet, shine soles
on the wide bristles of cilia.

conjunctiva

a mucous mitten,
it lines the inner,
secretes the off–white slush of sleep
drifting or swilling
into blind corners and creases.

lachrymal apparatus

the salivary glands of sadness,
or shock, or sins that make us sick of our dusty selves;
here are the tears that squeegee sickness,
that window–wipe insects,
that wring out the worry from worlds we need,
with each blood–shot eye, to envision.

Eyeball

Lazy,
hammocked in fat,
membranous sac swaying enough to see

the sites it pivots sideways, the ball
follows the brain's bare code
back to its base or, sick of the system,
calls it names, quits, and closes.

Beneath the cool bonnet of the lid,
it listens to dark,
unclasps color from the iris,
skinny–dips in the dusk of the unconscious
that dives it down.

Though later it tries to rise,
tangled in nerves, the eye
meshes with dreams' murky mirages
and what is seen there.

The Nose

Its cartilage cave echoes with all that blooms,
births, buries itself or others.
On bone walls: begonias, basil,
skin scrubbed at midnight,
the underside of sand dollars,
mint leaves moldy in memoirs.

On damp days, stalactites drip
with the rhythm of rodents clipping
into stone crevices, into bat–sized cracks,
into snoring quarries where memory,
ever cornered by aroma,
huddles, shivers, sobs, surrenders.

Molars

Behind a cove of jagged stone:
crab claws clutching the red–clay shore.
The undertow of tongue
tugs till the sweet sea deceives its victims.
What is lured in is lost—
Scylla and Charybdis
easier escape than these
six crustaceans crushing.

Tongue

Its tip is the trickiest twist
        of talk. Thought unknotted.
                The curl of conversation caught
                        and compromised between teeth.
                                Frenulum clipped, it flips
                                about like an animal skimmed
                                not shot. Near death, its syllables singe,
                                catapult past lips or slip
                        into the dark unsaid, the long
                claws of the mute
        cat licking, licking, licking
its slippery victim.

Taste Bud

Flask of fine tongue filled;
a server of sense without the silver,
unstopped by smell;
snake charmer piping temptation
to the red reptile.

What shall we pour down the holes of hunger,
post to the lying sender of telegraphs

en route to a soured stomach?
How shall we boost up the bitter and bland
unbalanced by bad reviews?

Ah, designer of *carpe diem*,
you sit on a just–brushed shelf
dictating diet and drink,
ever the body's tyrant,
ruling so distastefully
with a rosy bud.

The Epiglottis

is stuck in autumn,
a lone, yellowed leaf almost lifting
into wind, hovering

on the larynx ledge,
in the throat's draft, ever in the shade
of your talking tongue.

Vocal Chords

1. False

Mucous–thick impostors,
they lip–sync the larynx scale,
deem themselves "superior,"
con *American Idol* with their delinquent,
amateurish fibrous band.

2. True

Falsely publicized as "inferior,"
vibratos too pure for Hollywood hounds,
their saints' sounds nip the heavens,
so holy in the operatic stream
of a sweet, melodic shower.

Esophagus

The shuffling–off–to–Buffalo, toboggan ride slide,
do–not–pass–go short slope to the stomach;
the tunnel of swallows and masticated morsels
bound for the belly, the bowels, and the bowl
on days when everything (boiled, spoiled, or fried)
in the choking world goes down,
the right way.

IV.

The Sacrament of Penance

I. Absolution
>   a second plank given to us
>   by the mercy of God after shipwreck
>   — Edward Pusey

Forgiven once—
and–for–all at our birthing baptism, we still
circle high seas, forget to breathe
the airy Spirit, go under
and under.

Our collared step–father
sights us as stranded, locates sorrow
in those lost cells circling
each drowning mouth. He too
is wet from shipwreck,
a servant–sailor soaked to his mortal skin,
but sanctified.

It is the Other who holds us,
first holding out
the long plank of His cross
to pull us in, let us drink again
his unsalty, preserving self.

II. Repentance
>   *the necessary preparation*

>   *contrition*

in the dark night of the soul,
no soul left. the blackness of barren bellies,
all that is shriveled, starved. in the dark night

of our sin, hell hovering, heaven's distance tipping into
east from west widening. in the dark
sight of our infested selves,
our soot–filled souls. in
sin.

confession

A Lazarus, dead and still dying,
I stink with the rotting
of sin wrapped tight about limbs
limp with what man is and isn't.

      by my fault,
      my own fault,
      my own most grievous fault,
      I confess that I have committed. . . .

A Jonah, slipping in the vomit
of what ingests us when we swallow
the direction away from God

      For these and all my other sins
      which I cannot now remember,
      I am heartily sorry. . . .

A Caesar's wife haunted by the hell
of what we are: gardens exiled, heels crushed,
crucifixions tattooed across our supplications.

      Wherefore, I pray God to have mercy upon me,
      and you, my father, to pray for me
      to the Lord our God. Amen.

amendment

Not the pillar–of–salt–looking–back–at–the–lack–of–limits scenario;
not the saccharine–soft–shoe–song–and–dance list of yes
and yes and maybe, possibly yes, I'll try, perhaps;
not even the pound of flesh sautéed on the scale with *Hail Mary*'s.

Instead, geometry's half–halo of inscription:
prick of the compass steel, the line from then to now
steady and bright and eerily even for one–hundred–eighty
contrite converted degrees.

Ash Wednesday

Fingernails scrubbed clean as latrines
in the army, this symbol
of a man dirties his thumb
with our sin, the powdery ash riding high
on his pores, not sinking in
before he sketches the gray
of our dirt–birth across a brow
we were born to furrow.

Listen to the sound of forgiveness:
the crossing of skin, the cult–
like queuing up to explode
in ripped whispers, "Lord,
have mercy; Christ, have
mercy; Lord, have mercy."

And we want it. And we take it
home with us to stare back
from a lover's forehead,
to come off in a smear on the sheets
as we roll onto each other's skin,
or to wear like a bindhi this medal of our not winning
each day we wake to the worlds
we are and are not.

And when we wake too early
before the light of just–becoming–day
sneaks in on us, and we stand, toes cold,
in the tiled bathroom, still lonely, deceived
into piety, scrubbing away the grime of our humanness
like fierce fierce toothbrushes on latrines
in the army, there it is still,
raw with our washings:
the human beneath.

Skin Rising

You say the bites are kisses,
that they swell
toward heaven white,
red about the edges, sucked by
angels, their mosquito hisses
hesitating like his brother wishing
Abel wasn't right. This other hell
inside the veins transmitted
from one to one to one: the perfect legend
of blood, betrayal, suffering, and kisses.
We swat at such divinity; we itch
for it. The summer filled with misses
and mistakes. Behind the hedge
it's Cain alone who yells;
the angels bite his heels and his legs
then flap and flip into his eyes and nose.
The clicking wings that suck our sin and go
into another teach us how to sip
what starts out sweet, diffuses into dull.
These are angels whispering in my head,
the after–echo of the morning bells;
they tell me bites are kisses
that they swell into the mouth
and loiter in the lungs; the heavy wishes
settle in the liver, but the rest
become the face and soul, become the glistening
within the eyes. Now insect–like
we flit and lick and see about all sides,
our feet still sticky on each other's skin.
The wings are light and veil us from sin
that bites our kisses, kisses all our bites.

Divorce

"Because of the hardness of your hearts . . . "
— Matt. 19:8

The stone
thrown, the woman
at the well
well drowned, the
"go, and sin no more"
no more. This is what we pull up
with the bucket
of bitters,
our wine watered down
to wishes and would–be's.

This is where we fall
down the well–it–is–not–
with–our–souls.
No smooth sea to flee across,
no fish belching a rescue.
How hard can a heart be hardened,
flung about the necks of the thrashing?
How many sin–fulls of stone can a stomach hold
before the soul sinks? Fisherman,
grant us your granite
writ, your wet words of mercy,
as, even now, capsized and drowning,
we swallow your salutary ablutions.

Years Later: His Funeral

Children tug at the dark
folds of my skirt,
hands pink with just–autumn air.

They once huddled behind me,
hiding from the shadow of your arm raised:
swoop of a bird too large for the suburbs.

They cry as before they could talk,
for breath, dark, breast, the way we

cluster, move closer, want
to be gone, forget, not to forget
(my reasons, not theirs). Today, I want this dirt

but only to throw away, like ashes,
like confetti from a skyscraper
on a day when the wind could pick every voice from the ghetto,
wind it into the long wail of a hurricane horn,
warning us to go home, gather our loved ones together.

I've cried this day before in wishes,
fear, too long ago to matter. It is morning.
Among the gray, black, navy, someone else here
was your wife. At the prayer, I look for your scorn:
her face.

Feast and Famine

Montoursville, PA

I.
Oh you, who are barely a mouth,
I feed you yogurt, berries,
bananas, seven–grain bread,
broccoli, asparagus, gallons of milk
for your almost bones
and not–yet belly.

You who will suck
the good from my blood,
and multiply your round body
of cells, pursing what will be lips
for the earth's nutrients.

Kneel down now
in my larger body
before this unearthly altar,
the smooth circle of host encircles you
who are less than a sip from the chalice.
The priest is your father
and places his hand on our heads.

II.
Beside us on the rail,
a man grieves for his dead daughter,
clutches her framed photo to his chest
as he chews the wafer,
the only food in a stomach
that hungers for her.
And others at other churches
or far away from any cross,

will cry into their meals,
push away their plates,
their mouths too full of disaster to swallow.

What can we eat and sleep
but the world we live in
and the world beyond?

Body and Soul

Sundays, white covers
flesh; hands, those hungry graspers,
jut out, circle the silver
chalice. Once there, safe,
the Spirit clasps them, lets the red
stream into the small and cupped—
glass or lips, funnels to the stomach.

Hearts in our knees, we stay
down till words evaporate. Once, I stood
on the other side, robed, pouring out
my skin before I poured. Faces buoyed
above the surface of rails,
my syllables bobbing. Like the others,
I swim and sink alternately,
gasping for blood.

What catches
on the bone and clings
can drown us, tug us down
to sand or into a current thick beyond
the creek, the river, the open sea to Christ
parading across liquid so stiff it keeps us up, makes us breathe. Finally,
wine calms winds easily. I reach
out my hand, pour and kneel
simultaneously.

The Sacred   Heart of Jesus
O holy auricles,   venerable ventricles,
cathedral of cavernous sanctification, the nave we need,
windowed with the unstained wine of crucified corpuscles,
we echo in your vaults, our sin–cleansed cells rising high
into arias, into the buttressing arch of your aorta.
Here is the architecture of mercy,
shafts bright with agape shine,
our mortal veins split wide
on your unveiled
altar of
heart.

Eucharist

Host

the small circle of face
we see by
in light of wine

the sliver of why
that bends the bones
begs "Come!"

the orbed cross
bright in the palm
of the poor

the crucified moon
nailed high
on the night of tongue

Chalice

To sip is to sing the *Amen*
into veins, sweeten
the soured tongue.
But first: lips
pursed with it,
hollowed mouth brimming
with want.

This is the swallowing
of what spewed out: spears
stuck long in the side,
thorns thick in the skin.
No trickle.
A *Hallelujah*
torrent down the throat.

After the World Trade Center

At Saint Patrick's, rosaries run
two for ten dollars, medals two–fifty
while cameras click a rhythm
too quick for the cup and the pyx
six hundred feet down the aisle.

Saturdays, tourism tempts
even the timid in for a sneak
peek of the miraculous feast:
hope kneeling in strangers' knees.

In the center of the lens,
the world blurs
and bends. In its still
shot: host cracked, blood gargled,
tongue and throat pink and perfect.

On film, incense sins
the sin of omission, the *kyrie* isn't
in the picture, the priest
is dumb.

It is hard not to pose
for a postcard: eyes stain–
glassed, coins polished in the pocket.
The pious are pretty
in dim light, hands held out
for what we want.

Behind the back pews, two sisters point
their Instamatics; a man tips
his Mets cap; a woman loosens
her new–bought cross and watches the show.

In their random row, the kneelers look
too much like us.
We claim our *Mary*'s
as theirs, and snap our photo.

Outside and down
the street, the Trump Tower
shadows the sidewalk.

V.

Transplant, Transport, Transubstantiation

At four o'clock, he hops on a plane to Oslo
with eight pounds of eyes, sixty feet of skin
implanted in a hospital box.
The stewardess knows him by name.

From the tenth row, he waves at no one in particular.
   Across town
she waves back from her office chair,
later from the kitchen. She translates miles to meters,
Swedish to Dutch to Norwegian
in the middle of Egg–Drop soup. He

ignores his neighbors,
cuts into his Salisbury steak,
slowly rolls peas into a pile at 40,000 feet.
While he melts custard under his tongue, she's
humming the only song she knows on Zimbabwe,
hoping he'll chime in the refrain.

The box pushed under his seat has his feet on it,
is now in his lap, fingers tapping a rain dance
   she does not know.
(How tightly the eyes are packed.)

Good china: her hands won't stop
hooking and unhooking the metal clasps not
in the soap–gray water. Fingers wrinkle at the tips. Fingernails
   stay dirty.
"Open it!" she shouts as he crosses into a new continent,
feet asleep, wrist just inside the handle.

On the couch, she flips pages, scans an article.
She clips him for scrapbooks,
pastes him beside two obituaries,
a lock of hair, hotel bombings.

The clouds (livers, kidneys, mis–
shapen hearts, stomachs turned inside–out)
give him indigestion. He wants to be
there, done, coming back.

"Unfold it," she whispers. "Shake it out like a sheet":
stars and stripes of crisp cotton flapping
from the wings of the 747, cotton become skin
etched with thin maps fading mid–air in the rain.
Sixty feet to wrap yourself in, sixty.

He asks for coffee, wants rain.
She hears it for him: round, seeing, rolling off
wings and into towns with one, maybe two doctors.
Women in aprons clattering out to the streets.
Men in the middle of mowing. And children.
"Miracle," they're saying, skin wet with dew, "manna,"
palms flat, open as wafers.

Flight Patterns

July 17, 1996; Montoursville, PA
TWA Flight 800

On time, normal, through average air,
your plane came home to me
out of dusk above the Montoursville horizon
and settled without fanfare on the runway
just as, in New York, that other plane took off
to Paris with the neighbors' children
pressing their faces to the window to see
the last of Long Island,
their horizon waiting to explode
into sunset.

We didn't know driving home,
lugging your two suitcases from the car
and up our stairs to the bedroom,
the emptiness of other rooms,
the space on a pillow where a head should be.

Our first child slept soundlessly
in the room of my body.
We had just learned she was there,
the trip we would all take together
as yet unplanned.

What patterns are these?
Prayers for the unborn crisscrossing
those for the newly dead,
a strange radar of dread
hugging hope in the stomach.
Parents of the just–buried and just–begotten
circling a small town with their weeping.

Before I knew,
I slept, exhausted
by the small one within me
curled tight as a tornado
ticking its way to an explosion
I longed for.

Exhausted, too, from your travel,
you didn't sleep, but read
from the doctor's color brochures
our child's beginnings,
the daily care we must take;
then perched yourself
before the black–and–white news
and learned.

When you woke me,
your voice was the sound of small birds
flapping from the nest,
the hush of the watching world
huddled and blazing.

Somewhere in Yugoslavia

Somewhere in Yugoslavia,
we turned miles the wrong way,
I suppose the pig's screech tugged at our ears
though we did not hear it.

But there
the pink carcass hoisted up by the hooves,
the snout still twitching,
and you, re–sharpening the knife.
The backyard filled with dark–eyed children,
and a boy, a garbage can roped to his bike, waited for scraps.

You knew just how to do it,
sawing beneath the bones
like diagrams in cookbooks.

We stepped inches and,
somewhere in Yugoslavia,
a mare snorted, skimmed our Polo shirts with its cart,
its driver swinging his stick.
Then, rounding the corner,
a thick–mustachioed man stretching an accordion,
slick black–haired boys clashing pan lids,
a girl waving the flag like a fan.

Somewhere in Yugoslavia,
somewhere outside of ourselves,
for more than a moment,
we forgot the markings on our map,
where we were headed and why.

At the British Museum

Ninety degrees inside and
the mummies are un–creasing
knees, stiff necks; letting complexions breathe;
their two–inch strips rolled up surreptitiously
on scotch tape dispensers stolen last Christmas from security's
decorating party. Wonderfully fleshless, they smirk,
blink an SOS at us that says,
simply translated from the Egyptian,
"Distract that six–foot guard
while we stroll past to Elgin's Marbles;
it's larger in there and cold,
filled only with stolen stones
that now think they're English and wet
and, what's more, we've heard the guards
are bored and won't notice a few extra bodies
here or there posing as tourists." We obey as always
unquestioningly, unused to the heat and willing
to pacify anything dead.

The guard, an air traffic controller stuck
on tile, is half–
cooperative, exasperated
by questions: the Rosetta Stone,
the Magna Carta, and how to get
from one case to another,
so many clear rectangles to route past,
a Snow White nightmare of glass coffins, controlling
our weather of warm bodies
with what we should or once knew
in the hot seats of our schooldays,
sweating on desks and lunchboxes
and the open scripts of our thoughts.

As elsewhere, the un–bandaged are now
on their own—there is too much old here
for our old bodies, everything yellowed
pinned down like the unfortunate
monarchs who knew too little to stay
as they were and crawl
amidst the decrepit or decayed,
the barely formed bones
of our beginnings
stretched out for display
in the foreign soils
we've variously labeled home.

Outside, the columns wedge apart
cement and cloud,
keep at bay the crushing weight
of now, always, and afterlife,
while we maneuver to the Underground,
once again praying
we'll make the right choice
in the cool hollow of the tunnel.

Ireland: The Dispossessed

> Even today, those dispossessed by English landlords
> roam the land of their ancestors.

I.
It is the habit they don't dream
of exhaling nights when the gravel
of great–grandpapa's goings sits still
beneath the trailer's tires. Mornings the land
is again the flat sheet of their bed,
the sun's quarter testing its tightness. They are well taught
in the un–winding of time, the tucking in
of day's corners, the ritual of road and rest
connected to carburetor or cart
and the atlased eye of an ancestor.
It is enough to fix the sink, the fence,
the sloping barn of a farmer's
widow, but better to be the unfixed
view she watches out the window.

II.
Along the causeways,
clotheslines crisscross the road's shoulder;
officials roll in boulders to run the roamers out,
a rerun of the resurrection, backwards.
Signs posting fines for loitering
squeak: dispossessed winds.

III.
Unwelcomed now even at back doors,
some smuggle what's wanted
over the bold line of borders:
window glass, microwaves, escape for the settled
enticingly promised by VCR's. With their new miles

of dollar bills, they build in the best districts
wood, stucco, aluminum siding, brick
status symbols unlived in. Afraid of kin
and like–kind, they bar up
windows, live instead like kings
of the road in their new
dustless driveways.

Cape

What doesn't fit is
loose enough to move
in. Drape place on your shoulders and go.
Inflated: a map with beret,
your fabric–skin thick
enough. To twirl,
spin wind where the sleeves aren't.
Lift yourself. It's latitude you like.
Who says there are four winds
only? Fast–pitch caution. Breeze or
tornado—one is the other
sometime. You know where the sun is. Even melted,
you're a flat felt globe, tilting.

Seagulls

"The birds sound like a dog toy, squeaking." This is what she is thinking, sprawled in the backyard on a new lawn chair, face down toward the Indiana ground. She has never had a dog. The plastic strips curve out slightly with her breasts and stomach. She imagines, although she has always hated it, that this is the beach, that the schoolchildren stumbling along sidewalks have gotten lost, confused by their rumpled uniforms, and are coming, all of them, to her porch for cocktails and cheese curls the size of snails. The youngest one with the gray shell is her husband and doesn't like her in shorts, and besides, their dog, which is as small as a large–mouthed bass, has eaten all the garlic and is excessively talkative, not to mention that, as always, the tide is coming, coming, coming.

I know, of course, that the woman is I, even as I walk up in my uniform, trying to get the sand out from between my toes. But when has she ever recognized her own petticoat, uneven beneath the hem, or the dog in my voice? To her, I am the yellowest line of sun when the lids are closed. And to you?

Come. There are popsicles in the icebox and marguerites in the glasses. And what better place than such pink sand to sip and love before my husband appears and we shall, at high tide, have to bury the dog?

When She Moves Beside Me

From the corner of my eye,
I see her everywhere
bundled in browns: coat, hat, scarf,
her long braid heavy on her back,
heavy for her forty years,
or twenty, or fifty.
She turns her face away too quickly to tell.
It is just the curve that I see,
the fine lines, then the blur of form and face
staring away from the train window
whenever I wave good–bye.

It is the slight bend in her back that I know,
the slow turn around the corner.
It is the soft clap of her boots that warns me:
this is her street, her house, her life.
When she moves beside me,
one of us is gone.

Grafting

After the backyard opened up from lightning
(childhood and cherry tree split and splintering),
you chalked a shadow in the grass.
Each evening for two months,
you wound its blades around your thumbs.

But here the trees are sawed clean,
amputated at the trunk before I moved in,
the flat, scarred stumps staring up.

At night I see your fingers with leaves,
arms stretched tall, cutting into the sun.
Your shadow leans on the roof.

Breath clacks these shutters,
circles bricks, looks for cracks to slip
into. The ground is
something that's there. After a soft rain,
it feels like skin.

It's the wind that covers
holes the size of our lives.

This evening, no trees to hide him,
a neighbor came right up to my door,
picked up the welcome mat, and ran.

How It Begins

When his name, *Golladay,*
John David, tested itself on my lips
in the decrescendo of second—week roll,
he was dead, the morning
already old in its simple waking
of the world to loss.

Not knowing yet
how his car tipped into black,
or the screech that zigzags
parents' dreams, I was surprised only
by the lack of voice, his face
a hazy absence I cannot recall
still. The same week, a boy,

seventeen, just back from seeing
the Pope in a crowd of teens, a "good" boy,
hiked beyond the boundaries,
took too many steps along a canyon's edge,
and slid into the opening,
his gasp, a half—note of echo.

His father teaches at the college,
trained him to sing
Hallelujah.

None of us have time to pray
for what we don't see
coming, the blind
curve already twisting
into the hollow
undoing of sight and speech.

Today, during the change of classes,
the push and shove of traffic down tight halls,
another professor stood,
silent at the dual news,
barely nodding at words,
at fear in words.
His daughter's car flips yearly,
spins her around.

Though there is nothing more
to lecture, he will go on
to class. His daughter will go on humming,
driving on the edge of expressways,
along back roads, refusing
to slow down, to signal, to pray.

I drive away
thirty minutes to home;
on the back porch un–stack a bike,
tighten myself around its frame,
and push legs into the void.

There is a thin path spilled
beside the highway,
its asphalt, the long shadow of what cars leave
when they leave us
behind. It is not quiet.
The stream of engines mutter and whine
and want more. I go there. I do not look
at the cars, though they are right beside me.
I do not inhale their smells.
My tires crunch an uneven rhythm, tell me
how close I am.

After Learning of Our Own Deaths

I.
All day monarchs tango
right–left, tiger
wings dipping.
From here, nothing
to see but light and stripe. Orange
still owns this origin:
beauty, fear; fragile and flippant.
Even now, the sky tilts with it,
opens up its jaw.
The air is flapping
color and us
away.

II.
a flat night and a thin town

III.

IV. We believe.

Solo for Two Voices

Nights that I sleep, she bows in my bedroom,
mouth shaping our name,
stretches wide her lips,
starts her scales, then listens:
my aunt, at eighty, in a scab–brown building.

She sings each letter,
soars into an aria.
Vowels hollow around her, quiver—
her breath too small a wind.

Heart, throat, voice, note;
finger tracing air,
lifeline taut across ribs
like sound split into Eve, bone:
two lungs, two palms
pricked by the splinters.

In her sleep, she half–smiles,
curls around her roommate,
deaf–mute; sings away everything.
Perfect key. No words.

The air won't hold her long
much longer. Breath. *Pianissimo*. Rests.
In her measures, I hum our name *adagio*,
follow her eyes to a season I've never seen:
gold trees clanging;
grapes, blood–red, on the vine.

My Mother Gives Me a Tape of
My Father's Dance Band

My dead father plays boogie–woogie
throughout the house. Even in the back
yard, emptying the garbage, I hear his hands,
sixteen and agile, thumping, plinking, and do–wopping
along the thin tape that whirs in its recorder. What years
wind up in that casing, in the canal of my ear, in the curving aorta
pumping out his beat in my veins, in this aging staff of a body.
At sixty he still loved
his songs and stretched a broken pinkie to hit the notes.
My hands only snap and tap,
the bones bumping up against age. Still,
underneath flesh I know
something's jumping. Joy cracks
his rhythm in notes too strong to stay
in the grave, too staccato to listen
to sounds good–daying
in the bass of a previous page,
two–stepping still, though long
long since played.

Old Tunes

"Oh, where have you been, Billy Boy, Billy Boy. . . .
I have been to seek a wife; she's the joy of my life. . . . "

When the road dipped deep
and sky took over the car,
plastering each side of the family wagon
with southern Ohio,
and my father's broad grin
caught on the towns of Chillicothe and Portsmouth
while they sucked us in with their steel–mill smoke stacks,
small–town diners, and steeples slanted enough to let
the sun roll down and into the notes
that cluttered the front seat,
we three kids leaned and shoved and grabbed
at my father's songs to make them ours.

Bubbling "Down by the Old Mill Stream,"
we stopped to peel our socks,
wave them at passing trucks,
small prophecies of our victory
as we took the first steps
into the icy wet of his childhood
creek, not once letting go
of the wide hope
of his arm.

And later,
my great aunt's pastry stuck
at the lowest parts of our stomachs,
an awful weight,
we spit out "'Neath the Crust of the Old Apple Pie"
and other melodic jokes
strung on the shaky chords of my father's voice

from dance halls, summer camps, nights in the navy,
where he dreamed of the slow step
and fingers, smooth as a seductive dance,
that he'd finally find
years later on my mother.

Who was why,
those weeks in the car,
he bellowed and beamed
and zigzagged us into the summers
that smelled and tasted of song:
boogie–woogie and bebop, but mostly the cool blue
of Sinatra and Gershwin,
his one hand gliding across the wheel,
the other, over and over throughout our lives,
tapping his syncopated love notes
on the open heart of her palm.

Trying On

1.

I bargain for shapes, casings of what we choose for lives
between house and street. After years, not only clothes
look different; the soul tatters beneath them, or
newly sudsy, glows with the shine of bleach and promises
whose stitchings have come undone.
Listen how cotton rustles between legs,
lifts skin to another dressing.
I am somewhere between here and there
when arms start into sleeves
toward the past or future I've undressed from.

2.

In the small mirrored square filled with us,
my mother is pulling white over her head.
The dressing room is curtained with what will become
her life; the clerk is polite and young, and I am happy
in my mother's happiness, her dark head pushing through
the slim neckline of wedding.

And she is zipping up my back, the trackline of two sides coming
together always neater than what's expected.
She is beautiful and has chosen for me a black dress
strangely eloquent for the mourning
I wear simply beneath cloth.
At her second ceremony, I'll try on "daughter"
over the wrinkled fabric of childhood,
the shape of a house about me,
the past flannel of Father
in the old air.

Tape of My Dead Father's Voice from an
Old Answering Machine

He keeps telling me he's not at home,
that he'll reply soon. He doesn't know
he's lying, that what's hiding between the space
of words is space he's gone to. He repeats his name,
which is not the name I call him. I call him now,
hear only the unanswerable space answer. Home
is always where we've left, the space that means "before."
I know to keep his voice rewinding until the space
of now begins to answer. At the tone, I can't find a home
for how all space rewinds. Lying, I repeat that I am fine,
take out the home he was, and leave my name.